"This is the book I have been waiting for. bereaved I have been asked repeatedly by tho act? What should I say? and What can I rea answers in this guide to the world of the berea an equally useful roadmap for the bereaved th ty to their feelings. A quick and easy read, written in clear, compassionate and brief format, this small volume will fill a very large void."

—Dorie Beach, MSW

"This tenderly written book speaks to the heart of the process of accompanying loved ones through loss and bereavement. Attending to others' grief while honoring one's own can be a tough balance. . . . the writer speaks from his own experience, combined with the wisdom and lore of poetry, to address the essential issues of presence, compassion, and practical ways of offering support. It is a much needed addition to an area rarely addressed in the literature dealing with grief and loss."

—Chris Ingenito, L.C.S.W., Social Services Coordinator,
Hospice Care of Sonoma County

"This book tenderly touches every pain-swollen corner of a broken heart. This conversation incarnates the healing presence of God's grace . . . a gentle washing of the soul with hope, a telling of truth that restores the breath of faith."

—The Reverend Helen W. Appelberg,
founder of Community of Hope

"[*As Much Time as it Takes*] is a sensitive, insightful, and practical guide for anyone who finds themselves wondering what to say, what to do, and what not to do in regards to a grieving friend or family member."

—Marina Maimer, R.N., Hospice of St. Louis

"The guidance [in *As Much Time as it Takes*] for those supporting the bereaved applies to a broad range of losses, illuminating many points along the road to healing. The format is easy to read and absorb, especially for the bereaved themselves. The wisdom is evident in such phrases as, 'Let me have my feelings now. Perspective can come later.' This is one of the best books I've found in my 22 years of work in hospice and bereavement."

—Marilyn Traugott, Ed.M., Regional Hospice Program Coordinator,
Mercy Hospice, Redding, St. Elizabeth Hospice, Red Bluff, C.A.

AS MUCH

TIME

AS IT

TAKES

MARTIN J. KEOGH

A Guide for the Bereaved,
Their Family and Friends

Hampton Roads Publishing Company, Inc.
1125 Stoney Ridge Road
Charlottesville, VA 22902

434-296-2772
fax: 434-296-5096
e-mail: hrpc@hrpub.com
www.hrpub.com

If you are unable to order this book from your local
bookseller, you may order directly from the publisher.
Call 1-800-766-8009, toll-free.

Library of Congress Cataloging-in-Publication Data

Keogh, Martin J., 1958-
  As much time as it takes : a guide for the bereaved, their family,
and friends / Martin J. Keogh.
      p. cm.
  Summary: "A guide for the bereaved, their family, and friends from a
grieving person's viewpoint. Helps to navigate with sensitivity through
awkward moments of comforting those mourning the loss of a loved one.
  Articulates the overwhelming waves of grieving emotions, and assists friends
of the grieving to avoid clichés and find the right words at the right
time"--Provided by publisher.
  ISBN 1-57174-454-1 (5-1/2x6-1/2 tp : alk. paper)
1. Grief. 2. Bereavement--Psychological aspects. 3. Death--Psychological
aspects. I. Title.
  BF575.G7K48 2005
  155.9'37--dc22

                              2005015664

                          ISBN 1-57174-454-1
                          10 9 8 7 6 5 4 3 2 1
                Printed on acid-free paper in the United States

The friend who can be silent with us
in a moment of despair or confusion,
who can stay with us
in an hour of grief or bereavement,
who can tolerate not knowing,
not curing, not healing and face with us
the reality of our powerlessness,
that is a friend who cares.

—Henri Nouwen, *Out of Solitude*

To the memory of my parents

Linda and John
and
"Grillo"—Mi amorcito

Table of Contents

Acknowledgments

This book would not exist if it were not for Kristelle Sim. Her unwavering support, straightforward feedback, and ability to get the manuscript to the right individuals are why this book is now in your hands. At Hampton Roads, my appreciation goes to Lisette Larkins who understands how to persevere when something resonates as true. My long-distance editor, Elianne Obadia, helped give this book its form and poetry—she truly is the Writer's Midwife.

The following friends had the generosity to not be shy in their feedback: Byron Brown, Dharam Kaur Khalsa, Liz Rozner, Mary Ford, Owen Jones, and Zann Erick.

Many people read the manuscript in the early stages and gave their comments. I'll mention them here along with those friends whose steadfast belief in the book kept me writing: Anne Aronov, Anne Kilcoyne, Chris Ingenito, Clover Catskill, Cynthia Sterling, Dawn Banghart, Dorie Beach, Elizabeth Alach, Gretchen Spiro, Helena Worthen, Jillaine Smith, Karen

Roeper, Kate Murdoch, Ken and Barbara Luboff, Kirk Andrews, Leigh Hollowgrass, Loie Rosencrantz, Marion and Russ Archibald, Mary Herzog, Michael Steinberg, Nina Keogh, Pakina Fernandez, Paulina Hawkins, Peter Rosselli, Ray Landes, Rita Krug, Tony Jerez, and Wendy Fox.

And for the constant spark of life I'm grateful to my wife, Liza Keogh.

Introduction

Do you know someone who is bereaved? Do you wish to reach out to that person? This book is filled with practical and heartfelt ways to support people you care for who have lost a loved one.

If you're bereaved yourself, this book can help you more clearly appreciate and articulate your feelings and needs during this time that may be difficult and overwhelming.

I began writing this guide shortly after losing three loved ones in quick succession. My mother died after a four-year struggle with breast cancer. Shortly after her death, my father died of a sudden heart attack. His death was followed by a close friend being killed in a car collision.

As I was grieving these deaths, I recognized that many people were uncomfortable being with me as I experienced such life-changing losses. I also realized the errors I made in the past while trying to console friends who were mourning.

The skills and rapport we need to support the bereaved are rarely taught to us at home or at school. Yet eventually we are all called on to have this knowledge, sometimes when we least expect it.

So, as a step toward accepting all I was going through, I began writing this guide. As I wrote, I came to a deeper understanding of how extremely personal grieving is to each individual. It became clear that for this book to have value for people, it would need the input of many voices.

A diverse group of laypeople and professionals generously gave their time to this project. My profound appreciation goes to those who agreed to be interviewed and to all who offered feedback on the manuscript. These include hospice workers, grief therapists, midwives, priests, palliative care nurses, and many, many people who recently had someone close to them die. I also found a reservoir of information—and surprisingly, some consolation—communicating on the Internet.

My mother, Linda, was a passionate artist who cherished being the center of attention. She loved to cook, to eat, to create, and to receive praise. My father, John, was a lifelong athlete, and a dignified and reserved man. He had a sense of humor that held no punches and a great fondness for language and leisure. My friend Grillo loved people—and people loved her. She could disarm a bureaucrat, a mean-ass biker, or a close friend with her presence and smile.

I've written this book as a tribute to the vitality and love these three exuded and to the important roles they played in so many people's lives.

But this book is not about them, nor is it about me. It's written in the first person, but it's not *my* voice. While this book addresses the family and friends of the bereaved, if someone close to *you* has died, these words can help you acknowledge your feelings and needs during the different stages of your grieving and recovery.

If you find yourself in the role of caregiver, listen inside for the voice of *your* friend who has lost someone close. When you turn the page and begin reading, imagine that these are words he or she might be having trouble saying to you right now.

You can read this book in under an hour, yet the information and skills included here can help you deepen your relationships throughout a lifetime. The appreciation for your caring and support can come back and touch you for years to come.

M. J. K.

Prologue

My Dear Friend,

I have some terrible news. Somebody I cherish has died. I'm going through a difficult time right now and I could use your support.

I realize that sometimes it's hard to know how to support someone who's grieving. One day they need company and the next day they need time alone. Sometimes all they need is a friendly ear and sometimes a reminder to eat.

It's so easy to do or say something that can hurt a bereaved person, that it's often challenging and confusing to know when and how to help.

So I've drawn this map for you, my friends. With all that's happened, it's difficult to ask for support. That's why I'm giving you this little guide.

Nothing in here takes a huge effort. I certainly don't want you to do anything that doesn't come from your love for me. In truth, most of the time all I need is the small reminder that you care.

As Much Time as It Takes

On the following pages, you will find many suggestions. Select the ones that feel right for you. You might be comfortable helping with practical matters such as coordinating the funeral arrangements. Or you might wish to lend me an ear and give emotional support. This book is designed to help you discover what kinds of support feel most natural and effortless for you to offer.

You'll also find some activities and clichés to avoid during our times together. Your sensitivity to this information will encourage healing.

With death so close by, each moment has become more precious. I'm grieving now, but I do want you to know that I care for you. Thank you for being in my life and for all you've given.

With deep gratitude. . . .

Chapter I

A Fragile Cup of Revelation

Our Jeopardy

It is good
to use
best china
treasured dishes
the most
genuine goblets
or the oldest
lace tablecloth.
there's a risk,
of course,
every time
we use anything
or anyone
shares an inmost
mood or moment,

or a fragile
cup of revelation.
But not to
touch, not to
handle not to
employ the available
the artifacts
of being human
that is the quiet
crash the deadly
catastrophe
where nothing is ever
enjoyed or broken
or spilled or spoken,
or stained, or mended—
where nothing is ever
lived
loved
pored over
laughed over
wept over,
where nothing is ever
lost
or
found.

—Thomas Carlisle

Sometimes I might feel embarrassed
that I'm grieving and so vulnerable.
I might become bewildered,
not knowing how much I can reveal to you.
Sometimes *you* might feel awkward,
not knowing how to communicate with me
while I'm grieving.

Sometimes it's going to feel
downright clumsy for both of us.

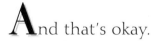

And that's okay.

Often it feels

as though we need

a license

to make mistakes.

This grants

(insert name:)

_____

a bona fide license to

feel awkward

or uncomfortable

while in the unfamiliar territory

of the bereaved.

This license gives you permission

to simply be present

to the best of your ability.

Chapter II

It Seems Impossible

(or: First Aid for the Recently Bereaved)

I sat in the garden spattered
by the great drops of winter,
and it seemed to me impossible
that beneath all that sadness,
that crumbled solitude,
the roots were still at work
with no one to encourage them.

—Pablo Neruda,
Translation by Alastair Reid

I've just learned of the death of my loved one.
I don't want to be treated like someone
who's infirm or bedridden.
But sometimes the smallest tasks
feel overwhelming right now.

You might ask:
Is there anything I can do?

In this state I'm often not sure
what I want or need.
If I'm unable to answer you—
and this is likely—
please offer something specific.

I want to help you understand
what I'm going through.
Sometimes it's overwhelming for me
to live with this much emotion
(or numbness).
You don't need to get overwhelmed as well.
As you read the suggestions in these chapters,
please remember you don't have to do
everything.
These are choices.
If you're so moved,
select what feels natural for you.
These are the kindnesses
I'll appreciate most.

I'm emotionally exhausted.

Sometimes I'm forgetful.

Small details seem overwhelming.

Tell me this is natural

for someone who has just suffered

this kind of loss.

If it feels like the right time,

embrace me.

And don't feel rejected

if I shy away from physical contact.

The touch might evoke emotions

I'm not ready for right now.

It's okay to try again later.

You might:

- Hold my hand
- Wrap your arm around my shoulder
- Hug me tight
- Let me rest my head on your shoulder

Healing from an emotional injury
can be similar
to mending
from a physical injury.

Encourage me to get enough sleep.
Remind me to eat
(unless you see me suppressing
my feelings by overeating).
Urge me to drink lots of water.

Feel free to bring over food.

Especially, homemade food

that only needs to be heated and served.

I especially have a hankering

for comfort foods:

- homemade chicken soup
- macaroni and cheese
- warm tapioca
- mashed potatoes
- anything creamy

Ask me about my personal favorites.

The foods I enjoyed while growing up

may be indigenous to other cultures.

Or I may have special dietary needs.

I'm having trouble
telling people about my loss.
On top of my own tidal waves
of emotion (or numbness),
I have to deal with
other people's reactions
and discomfort.

You could really help
by offering to make phone calls
so that I don't need
to be the first
to tell people the news.

You might offer

to sleep over

so I don't feel isolated

(especially if I live alone).

Or, if it works for you,

tell me I can call you anytime—

day or night.

If I have children,
offer to spend time with them.
I might need someone responsible
to take care of them
until I am better able to function.
I may need to rest and grieve alone,
knowing that my children
are in safe hands.

But please understand
that if one of my children has died,
I might not want anybody else
to take care of my surviving children
for a while.

See if I've taken care of business.
Ask me if I've paid my utility bills
or if I have any other pressing
financial obligations to handle.
Have I let them know at work
that I won't be coming in?

Do I have appointments
that need to be changed or canceled?
You might offer to handle
some of my paperwork
or return phone calls.

I can feel overwhelmed

by having to take care of so many details.

If you're skillful at making arrangements

you might offer to help

with some of these tasks.

- Making plans with the funeral home
- Arranging for the death certificate
- Inviting people to the funeral
- Helping to greet people and keeping
  a list of all who attend or call
- Housesitting during the funeral
  to prevent robberies (thieves some
  times rob homes during funerals)
- Arranging transportation and
  housing for people from out of town
- Helping me with correspondence
  and thank you notes

Or perhaps you could offer to help with

- shopping for groceries
- mowing the lawn
- walking the dog
- doing the laundry
- driving me to appointments
- the gardening and household tasks

Marking this passage by a memorial
or tribute to celebrate the person's life
can be an important part
of the grieving process.
It allows me to more fully realize
that the person is gone
and gives me the opportunity
to say good-bye.

Please respect my religious
or spiritual traditions
and those of family and friends
during the funeral
and the mourning period.

If we are at a loss

for ideas for the service,

you could gently suggest that we

- encourage people to share stories about the person
- read letters from friends and family and the person who has died
- don't exclude telling jokes and tenderly "roasting" the person
- sing his favorite songs
- play videos and audio tapes
- make available personal mementos, letters, and photographs

If you don't see it

on my bedside table,

see if you can find me the book:

How to Survive the Loss of a Love.*

It will help support me

at whatever stage of grieving

I'm in.

---

*By Melba Colgrove, Harold H. Bloomfield, & Peter McWilliams, Prelude Press: 1991; 1993 paperback.

Chapter III

As Much Time as It Takes

The heart is a leisurely muscle. It differs from all other muscles. How many push-ups can you make before the muscles in your arms and stomach get so tired that you have to stop? But your heart muscle goes on working for as long as you live. It does not get tired, because there is a phase of rest built into every single heartbeat. Our physical heart works leisurely.

And when we speak of the heart in a wider sense, the idea that life-giving leisure lies at the very center is implied. Never to lose sight of that central place of leisure in our life would keep us youthful. Seen in this light, leisure is not a privilege but a virtue. Leisure is not the privilege of a few who can afford to take time, but the virtue of all who are willing to give time to what takes time—to give as much time as a task rightly takes.

—Brother David Steindl-Rast

In my grandparents' day,
there was more support for grieving.
Many generations of the family
gathered together.
People wore black for a time
after a person's death.
Often there were wakes in the home.
Now I'm expected back at work in a few days.
People expect me to be "fully functional."
The small reminder that I'm grieving
and may need to slow down
and heal goes a long way.
Encourage me to go at my own pace.
Keep reminding me of the importance of
putting my own needs before
other people's expectations.

It's often too easy for me
to get caught up
in other people's rhythms and needs.
You might see people smothering me
with an excess of well-intentioned kindness.

Please play "interference" for me.
If some *yakkety-yak* comes up
and starts overwhelming me
with chatter,
come and engage them
so I can slip away.

Encourage me
not to make
any big decisions
for a while.

A big enough
life change
has already
taken place.

I have so much going on inside,

that when you're with me

you don't need to do much.

I probably feel most comfortable

when you give off a calm,

relaxed air that leads me to feel

- there's plenty of time
- there's no rush
- I can take the space I need
  to feel what needs to be felt

When we're together,

make it easy for yourself:

Most times you don't have to *do* anything.

Just your presence makes me feel better.

If it seems

I'm keeping myself

unusually busy . . .

If you see me running around

most of the time . . .

If I'm numb . . .

If I'm having trouble crying . . .

Invite me over

for a lazy afternoon or evening

where we don't do much.

Offer to run me a bath.

Or we can watch a sad movie,

or listen to some sad music.*

---

*Some people who have suffered a big loss discover a sudden and mysterious appreciation for country and western music!

Come and hang out in my home—
maybe not even in the same room.

We can sit and read together.

Cook a meal.

Talk in candlelight.

Nothing special.

And let's keep the TV off.

At times
I may simply need
the house to myself
or an afternoon to walk alone
in the woods.

Help me preserve
some intervals for solitude.

Encourage me
to put aside times
in my calendar
for dates with myself.

Take me out into nature.
The majesty of nature
can help bring comfort
and take me to that deep,
wordless place
where I can see my loss
from a larger perspective.

Invite me to

- walk barefoot on the beach
- absorb the stillness and
  silence of a desert
- watch a sunset from high up
  on the edge of a canyon
- lie down and gaze at the Milky Way

Please don't try to save me

from my feelings.

By truly going through

all the feelings that arise

with losing a dear one,

I'm being brought more deeply

into my life.

I'm also being asked

to look squarely

into the face

of my own death.

From a spiritual point of view,
this can be an important
time for me.

Gently encourage me
to take my time
with every aspect
of this process and
to live each stage fully.

Chapter IV

A Gentle and Tender Hand

When we honestly ask ourselves which person in our lives means the most to us, we often find that it is those who, instead of giving much advice, solutions, or cures, have chosen rather to share our pain and touch our wounds with a gentle and tender hand.

—Henri Nouwen, *Out of Solitude*
(Notre Dame, Ind.: Ave Maria Press, 2004)

I might feel reserved and insecure
when you first visit or call.
I may not be sure of your intentions.

Please try not to arrive
with some big plan.
The first, important step for me
is to establish an unafraid,
heartfelt communication.

Look for my cues, let me lead.

I may not know what I want,

but I'm quickly aware

of what I don't want;

please look for signs of my resistance

and respect them.

When you make an offer,

always give me the option

of something else,

or of nothing at all.

Some days I don't want to *do* anything.

If you're having trouble
picking up my cues, try this:
Take a moment and imagine yourself
in my place.

Imagine that you've had this loss
and what you might be feeling.
Imagine what you might need
from those around you.
You may find you simply desire
love and acceptance.

In your own way,

tell me that you love me.

And why.

Talk to me

about my strengths.

Remind me

of my good qualities.

Send me cards, faxes, e-mails,
telegrams, flowers.
Remind me that you care.
Write me a love letter.
Tell me what you remember
about the person who has died.

Sometimes it just takes
too much effort for me
to telephone you.
Call me regularly and leave messages
(and remind me I don't need
to return your calls).
If you feel like you might be
calling too much: ask me.

Find out when it's hardest for me.

Quite likely,

it is Saturday evenings

or Sundays.

Invite me over.

Ask me what I'd like to do,

and if I'd like anyone else to join us.

With so much going on,
I might be forgetting my body.
Encourage me to get exercise.

Join me in some quiet stretching
to bring me *home*.
Or join me in some activities
that get my body moving,
my blood pumping,
and my sweat flowing.

Offer to massage my feet

or hands.

Rub my shoulders.

Ask if I would like a full massage

from you or from a professional.

Offer to arrange the appointment for me

if I keep putting it off.

My sex drive might drop

for a while.

Or it may go up.

If we have a sexual relationship,

please be sensitive.

Opening up sexually

at this time

may make me feel

especially vulnerable.

I may cry when we make love.

Help me to surround myself
with beauty.

Support me in keeping my personal
environment peaceful and harmonious.

- ask me what colors I feel good
  wearing
- fill my kitchen with flowers
- find out if I'd like to go a museum,
  an art gallery, or a sculpture garden
- find out what music I like
  and play it while you're with me

Create a ritual with me.

It can be simple.

We can light a candle

by the deceased's photo;

- sing his favorite songs
- tell stories of when she was most
  sweet, courageous, rotten, funny
- write, draw, or dance our feelings
  about this loss
- call out his name
- chant, pray, or meditate together
- visit the cemetery or
  disperse the ashes together

You're giving a lot to me right now.

Please remember: *Take care of yourself.*

Know your limits.

Don't overextend yourself.

If you're deeply uncomfortable

around tears or anger, let me know this

and excuse yourself when I cry or rage.

Talk to your friends about any

confusion or anxiety you feel with me.

Take time away when you need it—

in the next room, out in the countryside,

or any way that works best for you.

Chapter V

Giving Sorrow Words

Give sorrow words; the grief that does not speak
Whispers the o'er-fraught heart, and bids it break.

—Shakespeare

I'm trying to understand
what has come crashing
into my life.
By wrapping words
around my experience
and my feelings,
I'm attempting to make sense
of a life that is
now vastly different.

May I talk to you?

Can I tell you my stories?

I don't know how to describe
what's going on inside me.
But I may need to try.
And it will take a while.

Ask me,
"How are you doing?"
when you have the time
and receptivity
to hear the answer.

Sometimes I might get stuck
in trying to be "appropriate"
or in trying to please you.
As we talk, it helps me
when I feel there's nowhere else
in the world you'd rather be.

Remind me that I don't need
to entertain you
or take care of you.
And if you can,
listen to what I say
with a calm and open silence.

Place yourself,

sitting,

standing,

or lying down,

at the same level

as I am.

Let your body be open,

your arms and legs

uncrossed.

Let yourself be relaxed.

Don't be afraid

of eye contact

(and don't force it).

If it feels right,

touch me.

It helps if you use little cues

to let me know

that you're listening.

Words, phrases,

and questions like:

- Really?
- Um, uh-huh, and oh!
- How did that make you feel?
- That's awful . . .
- What happened next?

These tell me

you're listening

and interested.

Questions that call for "yes" or "no" answers
can make me uncomfortable:

- Were you happy together?
- Are you hurting?
- Were you satisfied with the funeral?

Because once I've answered "yes" or "no,"
I often don't know what to say next.
Instead use open-ended phrases and questions like:

- How did you meet . . . ?
- Could you tell me about the time you . . . ?
- I'm so sorry . . .
- I can't imagine how hard this is for you . . .
- What was it like at the end . . . ?
- Tell me one of your favorite memories . . .

These encourage me to talk.

Don't pull me out of my feelings
with small talk.
I don't need to be distracted
from my grief right now.

But you also don't need
to put on an air of false solemnity.
In fact, sometimes a sense of humor
is just what's needed.
Humor used skillfully
often helps to bring some movement,
some levity,
and a deepening of emotion.

On my lead,

bring in some gallows humor.

And don't be shocked

when I make jokes

about the dead . . .

Sometimes

the most healing activity

is to laugh at death.*

---

*A man in a bereavement group who had been married for 52 years was about to travel overseas and take his wife's ashes through customs. He was trying to imagine what he would say if a customs official tried to open the urn. "If he sticks his hand in the urn, I'm going to have to tell him, 'Get your hand off my wife's ash!'"

Don't be surprised

when I surround myself

with photos of the person who died . . .

Or when I wear her shirt to bed . . .

Or when I go to the places

we visited together . . .

Or when I do anything else

that helps bring the memories to life.

Reminisce with me.
Tell me stories
about the one I've lost.
Bring him closer
by invoking his memory.
Allow me to tell the stories
of our relationship—
of the pleasures and betrayals,
of our adventures and misadventures.
And allow me to tell you about the hole
I feel here in my heart.

Try not to philosophize
or strive to make me feel better.
This devalues my feelings of loss
and makes me feel wrong for my pain.

I'm probably not ready

to hear expressions like these:

- Everything will be okay . . .
- She'll always be with you . . .
- Good thing he's out of pain . . .
- I'm sure she's looking down on us from heaven now . . .
- You're lucky you had so much time together . . .
- Someday you'll look back at this and . . .

When I hear phrases that attempt

to counteract what I'm feeling,

I sometimes get confused or upset.

I'm grieving, and the emotions

I'm feeling are part of the healing process.

More clichés to avoid:

- You must be strong (for the family/for the children, etc.).
- I know she wouldn't want you to cry.
- Well, life goes on.
- God will never give you more than you can handle.
- You should count your blessings (or any other "should").
- Now you can get on with your life.
- He's with God now.

Please don't try

to solve my "problems."

Stay away from giving advice.*

If I ask you for advice,

you might first ask me,

"What do *you* think?"

Or: "How do *you* feel about it?"

And please don't preach.

Just be by my side—

an equal, a human being,

a friend.

---

*If you feel compelled to give advice, advise me to accept offers of help from my friends.
I'm probably having some difficulty with this.

If we're both bereaved,
we can be an invaluable resource
for each other
during this difficult time.
Our ears can be wide open
with compassion.
Let's allow each other
to have our own timing
and individual styles of grieving,
even though we might be suffering
a similar loss.

Don't be afraid

to speak the name

of the deceased.

This is worth repeating:

Don't be afraid

to speak the name

of the deceased.

Don't feel the need . . .

to fill . . .

. . . the silences.

After some silence
I might want to say:
"You're giving me a lot right now.
Sometimes it's hard
to let you know,
but I'm extremely grateful
for your kindness."

Chapter VI

My Heart and the Sea

Lord, you have ripped away from me what I loved most.
One more time, O God, hear me cry out inside.
"Your will be done," it was done, and mine not.
My heart and the sea are together, Lord, and alone.

—Antonio Machado,
Translation by Robert Bly
(*Times Alone*. Middletown, Conn.:
Wesleyan University Press, 1983)

Tears are nature's balm
for emotional injuries.
Your permission for me to cry
is one of the most loving things
you can give me right now.
If I cry, I'm revealing the confidence
I have in you.
I trust you enough
to show you my vulnerability.
Remember that I won't cry forever
(and that crying sometimes
leads to laughter).

It's okay to cry with me.
However, don't *expect* me to cry.
Sometimes my tears are spent,
or I might be someone
who doesn't cry around others.
You might simply hear me sigh
instead of crying.

If you can't take my tears,
if they make you too upset
or confused, let me know.
We'll work something out.

From moment to moment,

different voices will rise up in me.

- I didn't appreciate him enough.
- I hate her for dying.
- If only I had . . .
- It's all my fault.
- It's all his fault.
- I'm overwhelmed, it's too much,
  I'm afraid.
- I'll never love again.

These voices are accompanied

by strong emotions.

If I trust you enough to speak them

in your presence,

please don't invalidate them.

Don't respond with phrases like,

"Oh no, that's not true;

you'll be fine" or,

"You did all you could" or,

"Of course you'll love again."

Acknowledge that this is

what I'm feeling at this time.

Recognize that it must be hard for me,

rather than telling me

that what I'm feeling

is not true

or that it will be different

someday soon.

Let me have my feelings now.

Perspective can come later.

I want to tell you

about our last days together.

About how we met.

I want to tell you I feel bad

that I didn't appreciate him enough

while he was alive.

I want to show you her picture

and tell you about the plans we had . . .

That she treated me badly,

Gave me lots of gifts,

was unbearably ornery.

I want to tell you I feel guilty

that a part of me is relieved

he's dead.

I want to wail, WHY?

Where is she?

How could this happen?

How can God do such a thing?

I want to shout,

No! IT CAN'T BE TRUE!

If I get emotional

and the words are not coming easily,

you can reassure me

with phrases such as,

"Take your time."

"It's okay."

Allow me to do most of the talking.

Feel free to ask questions

but have your own responses as well,

so it doesn't become an interrogation.

Once I open up,

please don't change the subject.

If you're getting overwhelmed,

let me know.

People often say to me,
"I understand."
This can make me angry.
Not even I can fathom
the depths of my feelings right now.
How can anyone else say
they understand
what I'm feeling?

Often it's better to say:
"I can't imagine
what you're going through . . ."
"I'm sorry . . ."
"I care . . ."

Hearing my stories might remind you
of your own losses and sorrows.

Share them.

When I hear about similar stories
and feelings,
it helps me to feel like I'm not crazy
despite all that's going on inside me.

But please be brief
so that I don't get pulled out
of my emotions.

Sometimes you might find me

quite angry,

especially if I have suffered

a sudden loss . . .

- I'll rage at the drunk driver
- Call the doctors "incompetent buffoons"
- Lash out at my friends who "don't understand"

If you can,

stay with me,

let me feel my anger.

This too will pass.

If I'm raging,
offer to accompany me
to the railroad tracks
so that I can scream
as loud as I can
as the train passes by.
This also works
by the ocean.
It's big enough
to absorb all my anger.

If you're feeling strong,

stand beside me

as I curse God

for the injustice!

For the loss!

For this death!

God doesn't need

your defense.

Sometimes what's felt inside

has to be said aloud

(very a-loud)

to be released.

Sometimes I'm going to be intense,

sometimes irrational,

and sometimes numb.

At times it's not going to be easy

to be at my side.

But remember,

I'm glad you're with me

as I go through this.

I *need* you here.

And I appreciate your willingness

to be at my side

even through the discomfort.

And remember to be sensitive
to your own feelings.

If you're uneasy
around my anger,
say, "I'm uncomfortable,"
rather than trying to distract me
by changing the subject.

If you feel anxiety or fear,
you don't need to pretend
it's not there.
Tell me.

This honesty will bring us closer together.

I welcome your feelings . . .

. . . but please don't get so

emotionally distraught

that I end up

jumping out of myself

to take care of you.

In the end, what you say
or do is not what's most important.
Your attempts to open up to me,
to be with me in a vulnerable,
sometimes uncomfortable,
and compassionate place in your heart,
will likely be healing for *both* of us.

It might take more energy
than you imagined
to be with me through these dark days.
But it can create a deep bond
of friendship between us.

Chapter VII

Bone by Bone

There is a pain—so utter—
It swallows substance up—
Then covers the Abyss with Trance—
So Memory can step
Around—across—upon it—
As one within a Swoon—
Goes safely—where an open eye—
Would drop Him—Bone by Bone

—Emily Dickinson

People often make

a hierarchy of dying.

They might feel that it's better

to die of heart failure than from cancer—

it's better to die of cancer than AIDS—

it's better to die of AIDS than suicide.

Please don't let your judgments

affect your compassion for my loss.

People need to grieve many kinds of death.

Perhaps I have lost someone to

- violent crime
- a birth defect
- a trauma such as a car or
  plane accident

  Or maybe I have lost

- an adult child
- a spouse who has been in pain
  for years
- a friend whose death is
  unexplainable

Your sensitivity and ability to improvise

with the particular loss

I'm suffering

is welcome.

If I've lost a child,

I'm in a particularly sensitive place.

We're not made to live through such a loss.

We're not supposed to bury our children.

This kind of loss feels different

from any other.

Please don't compare my loss

to the loss of a parent,

a spouse,

or a pet.

Know that I may be no less crushed
by the loss of an unborn child
to miscarriage or abortion.

I might be feeling a profound emptiness
at the loss of the *person* to be,
and the loss of my unfulfilled dreams
for *my* baby.

Some clichés to avoid
around the death of a child:

- God wanted another flower
  for his garden.
- Well, you still have _____.
- At least it was now and not when
  he was older and you were even
  more attached.
- God wanted another angel.
- You can still have another child.

If you can, be there

for my children and their grief.

Just like the time you spend with me,

listen to my children

with wide-open ears.

It's important

not to use euphemisms

such as "gone away,"

"left us," or "is sleeping."

These can be misinterpreted

and cause the child anxiety.

Let my children know that

my emotions of grief or anger

or withdrawal are about

the person who died.

Reassure the children

that they are not responsible

for my feelings:

"He's not sad because of

anything you did;

he's crying because he's unhappy

that your grandfather died last week."

Together you can create

little rituals of good-bye—

draw a picture, write a letter,

or blow out a candle

for the one who has died.

If I've lost someone to suicide,

I may feel guilt, regret,

and a profound sense of abandonment.

It may be especially hard

for me to talk about

what has happened.

Encourage me to talk about the gifts

and pains of the person's *entire* life

and death.

If you consistently hear me say
things like, "I'd be better off dead,"
ask me if I'm thinking about suicide.
If I say "yes," ask me if I have a plan.
If I say "yes," direct me right away to a

- therapist
- spiritual counselor
- member of the clergy
- suicide prevention line
  (look in the front of the phone book)

And make sure that there are people
to keep me company at all times!

If you see me retreating

into excesses of alcohol, drugs,

or television:

offer similar support.

If I own a gun

and you see that

I'm extremely distressed,

offer to take care of it for a while.

And tell me I really am

important to you

and that you'd never want to see

any harm come to me.

Put me in touch with individuals or groups
who have survived a similar loss.

You can locate information about bereavement
support groups on the Internet or through
your local hospice, church, or hospital.

If I've lost a child, get in touch with a
Compassionate Friends group
and have one of their members contact me.
To locate a local chapter, call: (630) 990-0010 or
fax (630) 990-0246. On the Internet at:
www.compassionatefriends.org.

Please don't pressure me into joining a group,
but you might offer to drive me to a meeting.

Chapter VIII

Water of a New Life

  Last night, as I was sleeping,
I dreamt—marvelous error!
that a spring was breaking
out in my heart.
I said: along which secret aqueduct,
Oh water, are you coming to me,
water of a new life
that I have never drunk?

  Last night, as I was sleeping,
I dreamt—marvelous error!
that I had a beehive
here inside my heart.
And the golden bees
were making white combs
and sweet honey
from my old failures.

Last night, as I was sleeping,
I dreamt—marvelous error!
that a fiery sun was giving
light inside my heart.
It was fiery because I felt
warmth as from a hearth,
and sun because it gave light
and brought tears to my eyes.

Last night, as I was sleeping,
I dreamt—marvelous error!
that it was God I had here inside my heart.

—Antonio Machado,
Translation by Robert Bly
(*Times Alone*. Middletown, Conn.:
Wesleyan University Press, 1983)

Now that some time has passed,

I have more vitality.

I can see signs of life everywhere.

This death will be a part of me always,

but I'm beginning to remember

the person with more feelings of love

than loss.

The world is a more inviting place.

I have more energy

for giving to others and to you.

Life all around me

(and in me)

is perking up!

There comes a time
when structure can be helpful.

Encourage me
to put some things
in my schedule.
Join me hiking, swimming,
playing tennis, or at a concert.
Remind me of my hobbies.

Get me involved in some projects—
especially projects where I get to help others
who are less fortunate than myself.

Bring over animals

and children

and plants

to keep me company

and to remind me

of life.

Keep sending cards,
even when it appears
that everything is back
to "normal."

In time you can send greetings
without referring back to the loss.

Please don't assume
that I have finished grieving—
weeks, months, or even years later.

Your support and love
are always welcome . . .

. . . however, if after a long time,
my life appears *paralyzed*
in grieving,
encourage me
to work with a counselor
or a bereavement group.

One of the kindest things
you can do is call
or spend time with me
during and just before and after
the hard days:

- birthdays: his and mine
- holidays
- the anniversary of her death

Why don't you and I

go out and have some fun?

Invite me to socialize,

perhaps starting with small groups

and working up from there.

Invite me out

to reconnect with old friends

and meet new people.

Offer to accompany me

as I head out into the world again.

I may need a companion

for driving to work,

attending church,

spending a day at the beach. . . .

It's time for some pampering.

Suggest something nourishing

(or even indulgent!)

that I might not normally do:

- dining at a fine restaurant
- getting a facial, pedicure, or manicure
- shopping for something special
- soaking at a hot springs together
- milkshakes, sundaes, ice cream

I'm more sensitive and perceptive

because of the range of emotions

I've been living with.

Inside, I'm opened up

in new and stimulating ways

to people, to nature, and to the world.

Now that I'm grieving less,

I have more energy.

This combination of increased energy

and heightened sensitivity

makes this an ideal time for creativity.

Encourage me to get involved

in artistic and creative pursuits.

Join me if you share my interests.

You know it's been a rough road for me.

Sometimes I've wondered

if I would make it through.

But with your presence,

your help,

and your willingness to listen,

every day I feel a little more alive.

I *am* making it through,

and you deserve a lot of recognition

for *your* kindness

and generous support.

Epilogue

This guide is almost finished,

but not quite. . . .

You get to complete it yourself.

Remember that you have a particular way

you demonstrate your caring.

Take these suggestions

as a framework,

and then express yourself

in the style that's natural for you.

You can trust yourself.

Sometimes when we're asked to help,
we're called on to expand
how we see ourselves as human beings.
By helping me with this loss,
you might have found
yourself changed.

My gratitude runs deep
for your willingness
to take this risk.

My dear friend,

How can I tell you how important your support has been?

You've been by my side through an extremely difficult period. Your caring and compassion have truly helped me heal and grow into living my life more fully.

I will never forget that we've shared some of the most vulnerable and intimate times that people can experience together.

Thank you.

I want to tell you:

I love you.

About the Author

Martin Keogh founded The Dancing Ground, an organization that offers conferences and symposia on gender, race, and mythology. He has produced and/or taught with Joseph Campbell, Clarissa Pinkola Estés, Robert Bly, Coleman Barks, Malidoma and Subonfu Somé, and many others.

After attending Stanford University, Martin hitchhiked 25,000 miles through North America and spent time traveling to monasteries in Japan and Korea. In 1979, he became a Dharma Teacher at the Empty Gate Zen Center in Berkeley, California.

For the past 26 years, Martin has taught interpersonal communication skills using the partner dance form called contact improvisation. He has led master classes, teacher conferences, and intensive trainings in 67 cities in 16 countries on four continents. He has been a consultant with Touchdown Dance USA, which teaches contact improvisation to the visually impaired.

Martin's writings have appeared in five languages, including essays appearing regularly in *CQ: The International Biannual Journal of Dance and Improvisation.*

In 1997, after the loss of three loved ones, Martin gathered information from professionals in the bereavement field, including palliative care nurses, hospice workers, priests, and grief therapists. This information is synthesized in *As Much Time as It Takes*.

Most recently, Martin was named a Fulbright Senior Specialist. When not on tour, he lives with his family in southeastern Massachusetts. He can be reached at www.martinkeogh.com.

Hampton Roads Publishing Company
. . . for the evolving human spirit

HAMPTON ROADS PUBLISHING COMPANY publishes books on
a variety of subjects, including metaphysics, spirituality,
health, visionary fiction, and other related topics.

For a copy of our latest trade catalog, call toll-free,
800-766-8009, or send your name and address to:

HAMPTON ROADS PUBLISHING COMPANY, INC.
1125 STONEY RIDGE ROAD • CHARLOTTESVILLE, VA 22902
e-mail: hrpc@hrpub.com • Internet: www.hrpub.com